Why do we dance?

25

Contents

Written by Ali Freer

Collins

1 Warm up

Have you ever heard a beat and found that your toes just start tapping …

Your head starts nodding …

Your body starts bopping …

And before you know it, you're dancing?

Perhaps you love to leap and twirl about. Maybe you like watching your favourite pop star dance or seeing ice dancers glide.

Let's get ready to be dance decoders! We'll look at some fascinating photos of dances from around the world. Can you spot any clues to work out more about the dances and what they might mean?

Why do *you* think we dance?

2 Work it out

Let's look at our first puzzle.

How do you think these people feel as they dance?

4

5

The people in the photo on the previous page look really happy! Even if we don't feel good when we start, getting moving can really improve how we feel.

They are taking part in a big dance event in New York. They are all doing a dance workout together. This is when a dance is specially adapted to be an exercise class.

Dance can be a fun part of sports lessons.

Feeling good

There are lots of reasons why dancing makes us feel great.

Dancing also brings people together. It can be fun to do things as a group!

Do you enjoy dancing more with friends than on your own?

FACT!
When we get moving, our brains release special chemicals that improve our mood. These chemicals are called **endorphins**. This is one reason why dancing can make us feel happy.

For some people, dance is mainly a form of exercise. Others take lessons in a particular type of dance for fun. They love the dance, and it makes them feel happy and healthy, too. Some popular dance classes are:

- tap dancing

- ballet

- hip-hop and street dancing

- wheelchair dancing

- salsa

- rhythmic gymnastics.

There are thousands of types of dance to choose from. Can you think of the different benefits of the various styles of dance?

Are you ready for our next dance puzzle? Let's go!

Which photo is ballet and which is hip-hop?
How do you know?

9

3 Top moves

Look at this amazing performance!

arena ◆◆ LOTTERY FUNDED | uk

Who do you think
the people in
the background of this
photo might be?

These dancers are **synchronised** swimmers. They work together to perform incredible moves and acrobatics in the water.

The people in the background are judges. That's because it's a competition – the World Championships, in fact!

Dance competitions can be small, big, friendly, just-for-fun or very competitive.

There can be lots of different **criteria** for judging, depending on the type of contest.

Here are some things that dances can be judged on:

- how well the dancers do in special moves and techniques
- how difficult the dance is
- how enjoyable the dance is to watch
- how creative and original the dance is
- how well the dance tells a story.

Can you think of any other criteria that could be used to judge a dance?

Synchronised swimmers make amazing patterns with their bodies.

International dance contests

In 2024, breakdancing will be an Olympic sport for the first time.

FACT!
Many people prefer the name "breaking" to breakdancing.

In breaking competitions, individual dancers or dance groups compete to show off amazing dance moves. These competitions are sometimes called dance battles.

What skills do you think the dancers need to take part in a dance battle?

Is dance a sport?

What do you imagine when you think about "sports"?

A definition of sports is: "games such as football and basketball and other competitive leisure activities which need physical effort and skill".

So, is dance a sport?

People have different opinions!

> I don't think dance is a sport. It's not a game like netball or football where you score goals.

> Not all sports are games! You can compete without scoring goals. Running is a sport, so why not dance?

> Dancers aren't athletes. They don't always wear trainers and special sports kit.

> Not all athletes wear trainers or team uniforms. Also, dancers train very hard, and they are extremely strong and fit.

I think the main point of dancing is to look good. That's different from sport, which is about scoring goals or getting points for being the fastest or best at something.

I think some dances are more about how they look and some are more about competition. Dancers can get points for being the best, too! I think dance can be a sport.

What do *you* think?

One reason this question matters is because it affects what types of competitions dancers can enter. At the moment, for example, ballroom dancing is not included in the Olympics, but some people really want it to be. However, synchronised swimming *is* included in the Olympics. Is this fair? Why do you think they include synchronised swimming and not ballroom dancing?

4 Jump up!

Time for our next puzzle.

What can you see in the photo?

How do you think the people are feeling?

What do you think the dance is about?

19

The bright colours, happy faces and energetic movements point to the conclusion that this dance is about celebration!

The photo is of Bhangra dancers.

It is generally believed that the word "bhangra" was first used for a traditional dance from the Punjab region of India and Pakistan. It is thought that the dance was about celebrating the harvest of the bhang crop (in English, this crop is called hemp).

Another theory that some people believe is that Bhangra was originally a **martial** dance. A martial dance is associated with war and battles.

Why might it be hard to know for sure what the dance's history is?

Bhangra dancers often wear brightly coloured clothes.

There are lots of reasons why we might not be sure what the origin story of a dance is: sometimes people have told the stories through generations and things get changed in the telling.

Sometimes, there's one main name for a dance but there are actually many different versions of the dance.

Dances **evolve** and move about as people go to live in other places and take the dance with them!

Bhangra is an example of a dance that has evolved and travelled.

Nowadays, Bhangra has become very famous all around the world. Modern Bhangra is danced at a variety of events, including weddings and parties. It also features in **Bollywood** films. It's even a fitness craze!

Did you know?

There is a world record for the largest Bhangra class, last set in November 2018 – 4,411 dancers took part!

The drumbeat is very important in Bhangra.

Dancing is a popular way of celebrating all around the world.

Here is another dance of celebration.

Why have the dancers chosen what they're wearing?

What are they celebrating?

How would you describe this dragon?

25

Different places in the world have different stories about dragons. Sometimes, dragons are frightening and bad. But in Chinese culture, dragons often symbolise good luck.

The dance on the previous page is called a Dragon Dance. It can be a part of celebrations for Chinese New Year.

It is believed that the Dragon Dance was first danced during the Han dynasty of Ancient China.

FACT!
The Han Dynasty lasted from 206 BCE to 220 CE

Dragons are seen as powerful and noble in Chinese culture, and **legends** say they sometimes live in the water. The stories say they can control the water and make it rain when there's a **drought**. The first Dragon Dances were about asking for rain and celebrating **ancestors**.

Nowadays, Dragon Dances are often performed at Chinese New Year celebrations all around the world, to help bring in good luck for the year to come.

People from other countries also do "Dragon Dances" – this ancient painting shows one in Vietnam.

青安晥

黃龍盛世

27

Have *you* ever done a little dance of celebration – perhaps to celebrate winning a race, or scoring a goal in a game?

In the 2014 Football World Cup, the Colombian team would sometimes dance a brief salsa as part of their goal-scoring celebrations.

Salsa is a popular dance in Colombia and other parts of Latin America – as well as all around the world. It is a fun and lively dance and can be a mix of lots of different dance moves. The dance is strongly influenced by African and Spanish styles.

We've learnt that dancing can be a wonderful part of celebrations. Let's look at a different type of dance now. Get ready to look for clues!

5 Picture the scene

Here is our next dance puzzle.

There's a clue in this photo that can help you work out what the dance is about. Can you find it?

What do you think the mood of this scene is?

What might the purpose of this dance be?

31

The clue is the clock. It's nearly midnight. Can you think of a story where midnight is significant?

The photo on the previous page is from a ballet version of *Cinderella*. The clock is about to strike 12. Cinderella needs to leave the ball quickly before she turns back into her normal clothes!

Ballet productions can have amazing scenery and costumes that help to tell the story.

Did you know?
At first, ballet was just for male dancers. When it first began in Italy, women weren't allowed to dance in public.

Ballet is one of many dances that can tell stories. But what is the story of ballet?

It is believed that ballet first began in Italy in the 1400s. Like lots of dances, it moved around and evolved in different ways. An important time in the history of ballet was in France in 1661 when Louis XIV set up the Royal Academy of Dance.

FACT!

Today, ballet is a popular dance around the world. There are lots of different types of ballet, including classical and modern. Nowadays, ballet is for everyone!

In this production of Cinderella, there's a real pony and carriage on the stage!

Ballet dancers make their dancing look effortless. However, they have to train very hard and build up incredible strength to be able to dance as they do. Professional ballet dancers wear special clothing and practise in studios.

pointe shoes

mirror

barre

tutu

special "sprung" floor

Telling stories

Another fascinating dance that involves telling stories is a classical Indian dance called Bharatanatyam. In this dance, the expressions on the dancers' faces and their hand **gestures** are very important for showing meaning.

The dances tell important stories from ancient Indian texts.

"Growing up in England, learning Indian Classical Dancing has helped me to understand more about my Indian culture. I especially enjoy performing on stage!"
Vaishnavee Madden – doctor and Bharatanatyam dancer

6 Take a stand

For our last dance puzzle, we are going to look at something a bit different.

Who could these people be?

37

The people in the photo on the previous page are all wearing matching clothes. That is because they are part of a sports team. They are from the New Zealand rugby team known as the All Blacks.

They look quite fearsome, don't they? Their fists are clenched. Their knees are bent. Their faces are scrunched up!

These sportsmen are performing a haka dance before a World Cup rugby game. Can you guess why?

They are dancing as a show of team power and strength. Perhaps they also want to scare the other team! How would you feel if you were facing them?

The haka is a traditional Māori dance. The Māori people were very early settlers to New Zealand.

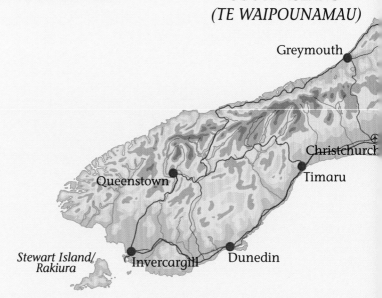

SOUTH ISLAND (TE WAIPOUNAMAU)

Greymouth

Christchurch

Timaru

Queenstown

Stewart Island/ Rakiura

Invercargill

Dunedin

Kaitaia

Whangarei

Great Barrier
Island

NORTH

Auckland

**NORTH ISLAND
(TE IKA-A-MĀUI)**

Hamilton

Tauranga

New Plymouth

Taupo

Gisborne

Wanganui

Napier

Nelson

Palmerston North

WELLINGTON

enheim

NEW ZEALAND

The sun god in Māori legend is called Tama-nui-te-rā. He had two wives, one of whom was called Hine-raumati. She is associated with the summer. She had a son called Tane-rore.

On a hot day, have you ever noticed how the air seems to shimmer with the heat? According to Māori legend, that's because Tane-rore was dancing for his mother. It was a dance with rapid, shaking movements. This was the starting point for the style of all haka. The dance can be about the celebration of life and creation, as well as battle and strength.

The New Zealand rugby team, known as the All Blacks, have made the haka famous around the world as a dance of intimidation. But there are lots of different reasons why hakas are performed. It has sometimes been to mark a meeting – either **hostile** or peaceful. Nowadays, haka are performed at lots of different events – happy occasions like birthdays and weddings as well as sad events.

Dancing for change

Did you know that people have used dance to fight for positive change?

A famous example is Katherine Dunham. She studied dance at college in America and got a scholarship to go to the Caribbean to study dance there.

When she went back to America, she set up a dance company, which performed and toured from the 1940s. She made up lots of modern dances, and she combined traditional African, African-American and Afro-Caribbean moves with other dance styles like ballet and jazz. She opened people's eyes to the beauty of dances from different cultures. She also took action to fight against racism, for example, refusing to perform in theatres which did not treat people equally.

She was famous because she was a wonderful dancer, and because she fought to gain equal pay and to show the different cultures through dance.

7 Cool down

And now ... it's time to cool down.

There are so many wonderful dances that they don't all fit in one book. Humans from all around the world have been dancing for thousands of years.

We know some of the reasons that we dance are:

to keep happy and healthy

to be a team or group, and perhaps be a bit scary!

to tell stories or make a point

to compete

to celebrate and have fun

But let's not forget – sometimes we dance just because we want to!

What is it about dance that matters so much to people, and makes them feel free, happy and able to express themselves?

It remains an intriguing mystery!

Why do *you* dance?

Glossary

ancestors people who were your family long ago, such as great-great-great grandparents

Bollywood the film industry in India

criteria ways to judge or decide something

drought when no rain falls for a long time

endorphins special chemicals in our brains that improve our mood

evolve slowly change over time

gestures movements (often with hands) that show what you mean or feel

hostile unfriendly

legends old and popular stories, that may be true or may be made-up

martial to do with soldiers or battles

pointe shoes special ballet shoes that help dancers stand on the tips of their toes

synchronised happening at the same time

Index

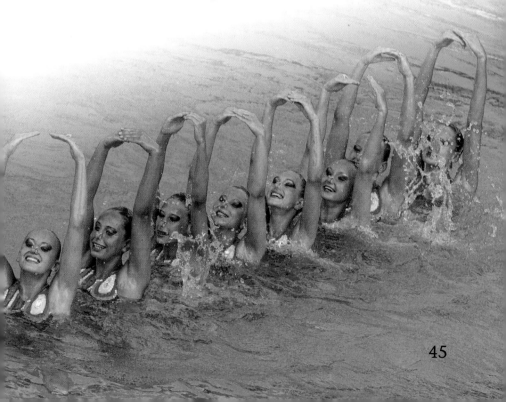

Why do people dance?

Use your dance decoding skills to work out why the people in the photos are dancing.

Ideas for reading

Written by Christine Whitney
Primary Literacy Consultant

Reading objectives:
- be introduced to non-fiction books that are structured in different ways
- listen to, discuss and express views about non-fiction
- retrieve and record information from non-fiction
- discuss and clarify the meanings of words

Spoken language objectives:
- participate in discussion
- speculate, hypothesise, imagine and explore ideas through talk
- ask relevant questions

Curriculum links: Physical Education: Dance; Writing: Write for different purposes

Word count: 2494

Interest words: Endorphins, evolve, gestures, legend

Resources: Paper, pencils and crayons

Build a context for reading
- Ask for a volunteer to share a dance they know. How many different styles of dance do the children know?
- Encourage children to look closely at the front cover of the book. Ask them if they recognise the dance on the front cover – have they ever seen someone perform something similar?
- Read the blurb on the back cover. Ask the group to think about and suggest the *meaning of fascinating dances from around the world*. In what way could a dance have *a meaning*?

Understand and apply reading strategies
- Read Chapter 1 and 2 together. Ask children to explain why dancing *can make us feel happy*. Encourage children to use the word *endorphins* in their answer.
- Read Chapter 3 and then ask children whether or not dance should be classed as a sport.
- Continue to read, pausing at the end of Chapter 4. Ask children to give three examples of where dancing *is a popular way of celebrating*.